The First 12 of Winter

Pictures by
Kevin Atkins

Words by
Nancy Atkins

EarthSpring Publishing

For Ryan, Christine and Kevin
N.A.
For Dad and Dakota
K.A.

Published by EarthSpring Publishing
Chelan, WA 98816
Text © 2021 by Nancy Atkins
Illustrations © 2021 by Kevin Atkins
All rights reserved. No part of this book may be reproduced or transmitted in any form or by any means, electronic or mechanical, including photocopying, recording or by any information storage and retrieval system, without the written permission of the Publisher, except where permitted by law. Inquiries should be emailed to EarthSpringPublishing.com

ISBN 978-0970574732
Printed in the United States of America
October 2021
First Edition
1 2 3 4 5 6 7 8 9 10

Dear Friend,

In the 12th month on the 21st day, you will wake up to the first day of winter. It is called the Winter Solstice. And there's excitement in the air!

The Winter Solstice is the shortest day of the year. And the l-o-n-g-e-s-t night. Starting the next day, however, the sun shines a little bit longer each day.

To welcome this return of the sun's light, all of nature has a party that lasts for 12 days!

(see next page)

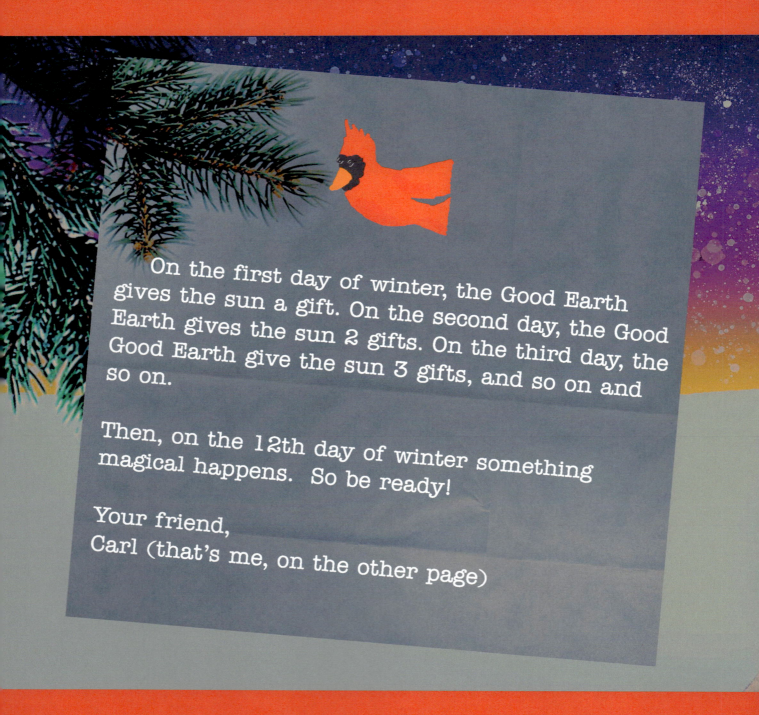

On the first day of winter, the Good Earth gives the sun a gift. On the second day, the Good Earth gives the sun 2 gifts. On the third day, the Good Earth give the sun 3 gifts, and so on and so on.

Then, on the 12th day of winter something magical happens. So be ready!

Your friend,
Carl (that's me, on the other page)

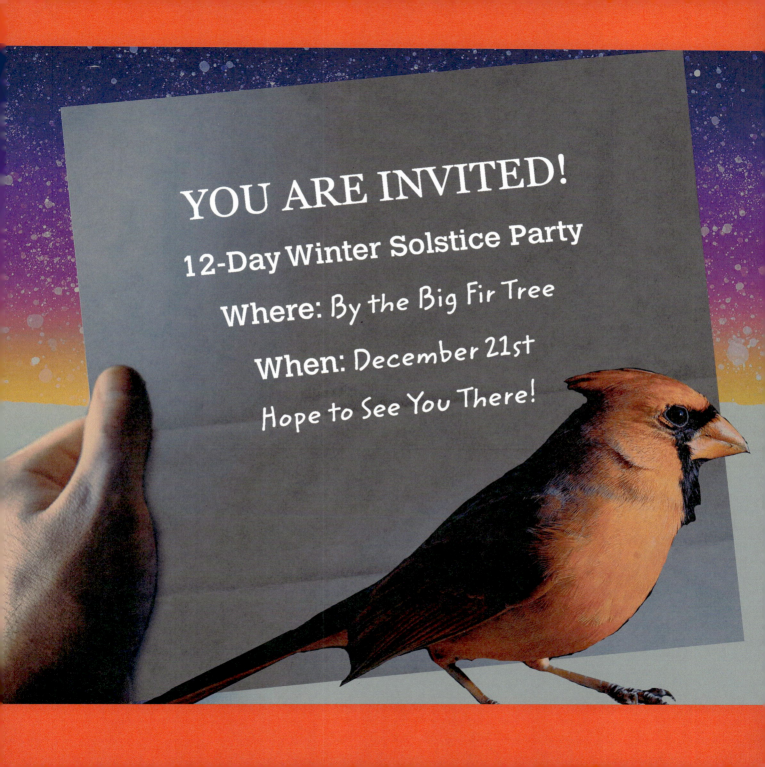

DECEMBER 22ND

On the second day of winter the Good Earth gives the sun...

2 polar bears and a cardinal in a fir tree.

3 caribou, 2 polar bears and a cardinal in a fir tree.

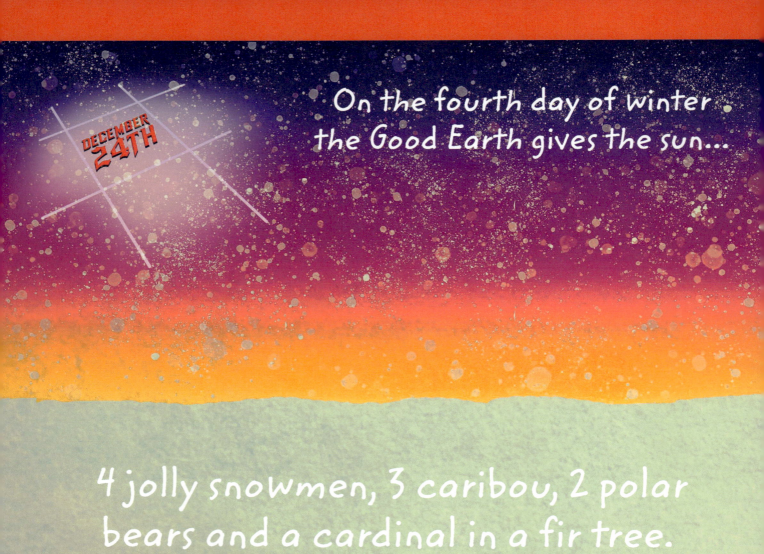

On the fourth day of winter the Good Earth gives the sun...

4 jolly snowmen, 3 caribou, 2 polar bears and a cardinal in a fir tree.

a 5-pointed star, 4 jolly snowmen, 3 caribou, 2 polar bears and a cardinal in a fir tree.

On the sixth day of winter the Good Earth gives the sun...

6 rabbits romping, a 5-pointed star, 4 jolly snowmen, 3 caribou, 2 polar bears and a cardinal in a fir tree.

7 salmon streaming, 6 rabbits romping, a 5-pointed star, 4 jolly snowmen, 3 caribou, 2 polar bears and a cardinal in a fir tree.

Then, on the twelfth day of winter, something magical happens.

Rising a little bit earlier than the day before, the sun gazes down on the wonderful gifts the Good Earth has given him. "What can I give in return?" he wonders. And then he has an idea.

Stretching his rays of light far, far out into the future he lassos 12 gifts for the final day of the celebration—12 months of days awaiting.

"Oh my," exclaims the Good Earth to all of nature, "that's a whole year full of magical days." And hearing this sends the...

11 barn owls hooting, 10 birch trees dancing, 9 field mice fiddling, 8 foxes trotting, 7 salmon singing, 6 rabbits twirling, 5 star points blinking, 4 snowmen skiing, 3 caribou prancing...

Made in United States
Troutdale, OR
11/29/2023

TIMBER! Talking Book

Scan this QR code on your smartphone or tablet for a free audio reading of this book with music and sound effects.